Chatham House Papers . 16

US Monetary Policy
and European Responses
in the 1980s

Chatham House Papers . 16

US Monetary Policy and European Responses in the 1980s

Kenneth King

The Royal Institute of International Affairs

Routledge & Kegan Paul

London, Boston and Henley

First published 1982
by Routledge & Kegan Paul Ltd
39 Store Street, London WC1E 7DD,
9 Park Street, Boston, Mass. 02108, USA and
Broadway House, Newtown Road,
Henley-on-Thames, Oxon RG9 1EN
Set by Hope Services, Abingdon and
printed in Great Britain by
Billing & Son Ltd, Worcester
© Royal Institute of International Affairs 1982
No part of this book may be reproduced in
any form without permission from the
publisher, except for the quotation of brief
passages in criticism

Library of Congress Cataloging in Publication Data
King, Kenneth.
US monetary policy and European responses in
the 1980s.
(Chatham House Papers; 16)
Bibliography: p.
1. International finance.   2. Monetary
policy – United States.   3. Monetary policy –
European Economic Community countries.
4. Monetary policy – Great Britain.   I. Royal
Institute of International Affairs.   II. Title.
III. Title: U.S. monetary policy and European
responses in the 1980s.   IV. Series.
HG3881.K5325   1982   332.4'9   82-11267
ISBN 0-7100-9337-3 (pbk.)
ISSN 0143-5795

Contents

Acknowledgments

I am grateful for the advice received while writing successive drafts of this study; it has benefited particularly from the help of Andrew Baker, John Kerbyshire, Craig Larrimer, Peter Oppenheimer, Joan Pearce, Richard Portes, Brian Tew, Tommy Thompson and John Williamson.

Rothschilds have been generous in allowing me to use research and secretarial facilities; and my colleagues in the international currency management team have been responsible, directly or indirectly, for many of the ideas in this study. Lesley Billot produced the drafts with an extraordinary patience and speed.

K. K.
June 1982

'Cecily, you will read your Political Economy in my absence. The chapter on the Fall of the Rupee you may omit. It is somewhat too sensational. Even these metallic problems have their melodramatic side.'

Miss Prism, in The Importance of Being Earnest, Act 2

1 Introduction: International monetary policy

US monetary policy greatly influences the monetary policies of other countries. The dollar remains both the chief reserve asset of most countries and the major currency used in international trade in spite of its periods of weakness in the 1970s. Furthermore, the close links between international money markets mean that movements in US interest rates affect interest rates and exchange rates elsewhere.

Changes in US monetary policy affect inflation and economic activity in all Western countries. European governments, which found difficulty in adapting to a weak dollar and to the consequences of a lax US monetary policy in the 1970s, are finding still greater difficulty in adapting to a strong dollar and to the effects of restrictive monetary policy in the 1980s. This paper explains the nature of the changes in US monetary policy and the ways in which they affect the European economies. The Introduction discusses the background to these complex interrelationships, and summarizes the chapters that follow.

US monetary policy is generally recognized as having been conducted in the early 1980s in ways that have been potentially destabilizing both for the USA and for the rest of the world. There is also a school of thought, in the USA as well as in Europe, that criticizes existing US policies even more severely. The present general deflationary thrust of US policies has, it argues, denied the US economy any kind of sustained recovery in economic activity for more than three years. The social costs of this, it is said, outweigh the benefits of any likely temporary reduction in inflation. Such a viewpoint has obvious similarities with criticisms of Conservative government policies in the UK.

The critics argue that much of the 'success' of US and UK policies in reducing inflation is the result of temporary reductions in inflationary pressures as commodity prices (including the oil price) fall in the face of world recession, as corporate profits are squeezed and while sterling and the dollar remain overvalued at unsustainable levels. A recovery in activity would, according to this view, be accompanied by a resurgence of inflation to former levels.

The contrary view — that inflation must be curbed on a lasting basis and that present monetary policies could, if continued, achieve this — is as widely and strongly held. Advocates of deflationary policies accept that such policies will mean a further period of little or no economic growth. If they did not believe that these policies are politically feasible over a period of several years, they would, presumably, accept an easing in monetary stance, since later reversal would undo much or all of the deflationary gains so far achieved.

It may be that neither view is completely right, and that some sort of compromise policy will enable the USA, and perhaps the UK, to maintain single-digit inflation together with a resumption of reasonable growth in the fairly near future.

This paper assumes that the present restrictive stance of US monetary policy will continue and that it will exert deflationary pressures on the European economies. The parts of the paper concerned with European responses to US policies are not directed at ways of escaping these pressures but at ways of adapting to continuing restrictive US monetary policy.

To speak of an 'international monetary policy' in this context is, to a large extent, misleading. It implies that the monetary authorities of the major Western economies formulate policies with some regard for their international consequences and after some attempt to reach agreement on objectives and methods. In the 1980s the most powerful of these authorities — in the USA — argues that it need not, and indeed should not, conduct its monetary policy with any objective except that of countering domestic inflation.

Nor, of course, are the major European monetary authorities particularly internationalist in their thinking. What they object to most strongly is the impact of US policies on the management of their respective economies. They do, however, tend to believe that domestic self-interest is best served by some attempt at cooperation both through such institutions as the European Community and through less rigid mechanisms such as 'economic summits'. They would welcome the opportunity to influence US monetary policy so that in its repercussions abroad it took greater account of their problems. In return they would offer the possibility of some improvement in transatlantic relationships and the prospect of greater support during any subsequent dollar crises. (After all, current dollar strength is unlikely to continue through the whole of the 1980s.)

US monetary policy determines world monetary policy. The scale of the US and Eurodollar markets drawfs all other financial markets. Even under a regime of floating exchange rates other countries have been unwilling or unable to insulate themselves against the rapid changes in US interest rates and the strength of the dollar. This dependence, self-evident in European eyes, is neither obvious nor desirable from a US standpoint. Both the Administration and its officials believe that the USA contributes to the proper functioning of foreign exchange markets by deliberately refraining from having an explicit exchange rate target and from intervention in foreign exchange markets under almost any circumstances (*see* chapter 2). The ending of US intervention in foreign exchange markets did not occur until more than a year after the change in the monetary policy of the Federal Reserve (Fed; *see* Glossary), and the policy of leaving dollar exchange rates to be determined by market forces was, presumably, more readily embarked on by President Reagan's Administration because it occurred in the context of a strong dollar. It is the policy of the Administration, not of the Fed, but there has been no suggestion by the latter that a more active intervention strategy would be appropriate.

The basis of the US attitude is easy to discover. It is a coherent part of a philosophy that holds that all government interference with market forces distorts market signals and increases inefficiency. This belief is reinforced by memories of sharp European criticism of polices that led to the long period of dollar weakness, and also of ineffectual attempts by the US Treasury and the Fed to fight market forces as the dollar weakened apparently inexorably during the 1970s.

The US view of exchange rate policy is probably not the result of its often-cited indifference to international trade. A decade ago that part of US economic activity directly exposed to exchange rate fluctuations —

the imports and exports of goods and services — was equal to only 10 per cent of GNP. In consequence, most Americans' lives were apparently unaffected by exchange rate fluctuations. That has changed, for today this trade totals more than a quarter of GNP. Comparable figures for European economies were around 50 per cent through the 1970s. The USA remains more closed than the European economies, but it is a difference of degree not of kind, and it is less marked once account is taken of the fact that much of the trade of each European country consists of intra-European flows that are not exposed to fluctuations against the dollar.

It is simplistic to argue that under a floating exchange rate regime Europe can direct its policies independently of US monetary policy. The exchange rate provisions of the European Monetary System (EMS), agreed in 1979, sought again to establish a zone of exchange rate stability in Europe. Arguably, in consequence, volatility against the dollar should be less significant since European companies, being averse to exchange risk, might turn increasingly to the comparative currency certainties of intra-European trade rather than trade with the USA.

This has proven not to be the case. In US eyes European perversity is exemplified by the way in which a decade of complaints about the weakness of the dollar has been succeeded by criticism both of the high interest rates that were necessary to halt that weakness and of the subsequent strength of the dollar.

Europe quite clearly does care about the dollar. The German authorities chose, during the second half of 1981, to push the dollar down against the Deutschmark through intervention in 'thin' summer foreign exchange markets. (Summer currency and money markets are 'thin' because turnover is limited in the holiday season and intervention — that is, buying or selling of foreign currency by a central bank to influence the exchange rate of its own currency — can have a greater impact.) The Bundesbank then made German interest rates lag behind the falls in US interest rates during the autumn to strengthen the mark. This too was seen as perverse in the USA; the Europeans had blamed the USA for high European interest rates but had then failed to lower those rates in step with the fall in US rates.

The reason for the Europeans' concern about their exchange rates against the dollar is that dollar strength has a direct adverse impact on their inflation rates which goes well beyond the proportion of their imports that come from the USA. This effect derives from the fact that almost all commodity markets, including the oil market, are dollar–denominated. In the long term, this may simply mean that dollar strength is reflected in lower dollar prices for commodities. Within a year, however, a 10 per cent appreciation of the dollar against, say, the Deutschmark translates into a direct 10 per cent increase in the price of some half of German imports and a very large shove for cost-push inflation. Conventional wage responses (indexation or quasi-indexation is the norm in Europe) lead to the perpetuation of such inflationary shocks. Again, from a long-term view, such impacts should tend to be offset by the periods of dollar weakness and to fade away but, given the acceleration in inflation that has characterized the world economy over the past 20 years, an unwillingness to take an Olympian view is understandable. (It is possible to argue that when a currency weakens against the dollar import costs rise, inflation increases, wages respond and a self-perpetuating inflationary spiral begins. When the currency strengthens against the dollar, the fall in import costs does not lessen wage pressures and so does not reduce inflation in the way that currency weakness causes it to accelerate. This 'ratchet effect' – so called because exchange rate volatility pushes inflation up without allowing it to fall back – requires special assumptions about the process of wage settlements and now carries little conviction given the depth of recession in the major economies.)

The nature of exchange rate volatility has altered since October 1979, when changes in US monetary policy began to cause dollar interest rates to fluctuate widely. Statistical measures of exchange rate movements at first sight give the lie to this. The standard deviation of dollar–Deutschmark exchange rate fluctuation in several years in the 1970s is little different from what it was in 1980 and 1981 – or indeed from the volatility likely in the next few years. (Standard deviation here has a statistical meaning, which can be interpreted informally as a measure of the average variability of the exchange rate around its trend value.) This measure, however, masks an underlying change that has made exchange rate fluctuations much more important to market participants than they were before the beginning of 1980. Through the latter half of the 1970s the weakness of the dollar against the Deutschmark followed a consistent, regular pattern; in almost every single month the dollar was weaker against the Deutschmark than in the preceding month. This did not necessarily mean that speculation against the dollar in favour of the Deutschmark was profitable; for US interest rates were higher than German interest rates by an amount which largely compensated for the depreciation of the dollar. If, for example, the dollar weakens over a year by 4 per cent while US interest rates are 10 per cent and German interest rates are 6 per cent then the total return on dollar and Deutschmark investments would be equal; or, looked at another way, the cost of selling dollars forward for Deutschmarks for one year, say, would be sufficient to offset the expected weakening of the dollar spot rate over that year. It is broadly correct to say that the forward market in a given currency against the dollar reflects the interest differential in Euromarkets between that currency and the dollar. Only indirectly is the forward rate a 'market prediction' of the likely trend of a currency's spot rate. In consequence, any statement about differences between the expected total rates of return in currencies is equivalent to the statement that a currency is generally expected to be weaker or stronger than its forward exchange rate.

Given this pattern of consistent dollar decline, foreign exchange and investment decisions were comparatively simple and, broadly speaking, it made little difference whether investments and trade were denominated in dollars or Deutschmarks. This was not only true *ex post*: the view that the total rate of return on Deutschmarks and dollars would be broadly similar once expected exchange rates moves were taken into account came to be widely held in the 1970s. In fact, frequently in the 1970s the Deutschmark was stronger than the dollar to a greater extent than the interest differential between the two currencies warranted. To continue the example above, if the dollar weakens by 7 per cent a year against the Deutschmark while US interest rates are 10 per cent and German interest rates are 6 per cent, then Deutschmark investments will be more attractive than dollar investments because the interest differential compensates for only part of the depreciation of the dollar. Again, looking at forward markets, it was worthwhile to buy Deutschmarks from dollars today for delivery one year out, since experience repeatedly suggested that Deutschmarks could be bought more cheaply in the forward market than in the spot market in a year's time.

It was in this sense that the dollar was 'weak' in the 1970s. The total return (interest rate plus currency movement) was systematically higher for the Deutschmark than for the dollar, or alternatively it was thought to be cheaper to buy Deutschmarks forward than wait to buy them in the spot market.

The 1980s have so far been very different. The dollar has been strong and yet pays much higher interest rates than the Deutschmark. Investing in dollars has become attractive for two reasons: currency gains and high interest rates. Moreover, the pattern of movement of the dollar against the Deutschmark has been broken, at least temporarily. During 1980–2 there have been periods when the dollar has weakened sharply, as well as periods when it has strengthened greatly. This has removed the old certainties underlying exchange rate patterns. Currency volatility as measured by the size of month-by-month fluctuations in exchange rates is little different from what it was at times during the 1970s, but the direction of moves is now unpredictable. There is no certainty that dollar weakness will offset the attractions of high US interest rates. Equally there is no certainty that dollar investments that are unfortunately timed will outperform Deutschmark investments. A German investor in dollar short-term assets in August 1981 would have found that, in Deutschmark terms, his investment would have been worth 10 per cent less by the end of the year while the difference between dollar interest rates and Deutschmark interest rates would have compensated him for only a third of that fall – a net loss of 6 per cent in five months. If he had continued to hold the Deutschmarks until February or March 1982 he would have had no currency losses and would have earned the much higher US interest rates – a net gain of 5 per cent in eight months!

Given the scale of these uncertainties, companies engaged in international trade and international investors (whether in the USA or elsewhere) can be pardoned for not being unreservedly in favour of the Fed's new policy. These uncertainties are felt particularly strongly by companies engaged in international trade. The scale of currency fluctuations in any six-month period since the beginning of 1980 has been sufficient to transform profits on export earnings to losses or, alternatively, to double or treble those profits, depending on the period chosen. This kind of fluctuation is unusual but not unprecedented (sterling appreciated in a way that surprised most observers in 1979 and 1980). While US monetary policy continues in its present form, this sort of currency fluctuation will persist. Given that most companies are averse to risk, continuing exchange rate instability on this scale may hinder international trade. Companies are increasingly using forward markets in foreign exchange to reduce these uncertainties. The Appendix evaluates their practices in recent years and assesses the extent to which forward markets can make trade independent of currency volatility.

As chapter 2 argues, the conduct of US monetary policy so far in the 1980s is destabilizing for the economy, for interest rates and for the exchange rate. The Fed recognized early on in its experiments with monetary targets that this was a danger, and has been acting, with limited success, to stabilize interest rates. However, the ground rules that it set for monetary policy will cause continuing volatility in US and Eurodollar financial markets until it ceases to give overwhelming priority to its monetary targets and at least partially readopts interest rate targets. This appears already to be happening to some extent: in both January and April 1982 the Fed acted to encourage markets to look through what were held to be short-term accelerations in the growth of the narrow monetary aggregate above the top end of its target range.

The volatility of US interest rates is their most striking feature on a day-to-day basis, but their average level since October 1979 has been as important. This has been responsible for the strength of the dollar. As chapter 2 suggests, there are two ways of viewing this strength. First, it may set the pattern for the whole of the 1980s — a strong dollar, low inflation and an eventual return to stable growth. Second, it may be a temporary aberration — present dollar strength has made exports uncompetitive and imports attractive and the US current account position is deteriorating rapidly, with the deterioration partially masked by the effects of the recession — and the price of present dollar strength may yet be a period of overcorrection through a suddenly weak dollar. The choice between the two is largely in US hands. The Administration and the Fed have a clear preference for the former path, but the question is whether they will pay the price for it once it becomes clear what the price is — a deepening recession lasting, say, a further three years.

Chapter 3 traces the relationships between present US monetary policy, interest rate volatility and exchange rate volatility. The present tight monetary targets ensure that US interest rates are unprecedentedly high on average and are more volatile than at any time in the postwar period (and indeed more volatile than at almost any time in US history). In consequence, exchange rate fluctuations are likely to continue on the scale of the past two years – and may grow still wider unless greater weight is given to interest rate and exchange rate objectives.

Chapter 4 describes European attitudes to international monetary policy and responses to the new ground rules set by US policy. The EMS does not have an institutional framework which enables its members jointly to influence their exchange rates against the dollar. Members of the Community have generally attempted to manage their exchange rates against the Deutschmark and, in effect, allowed the Bundesbank to determine their exchange rates against the dollar as it follows policies for the Deutschmark that reflect German interests.

The member states of the Community have complained about the high level of US interest rates and their impact on exchange rates and world activity. They initially viewed high interest rates as a short-lived phenomenon and expected the problem to resolve itself. They accepted the need to raise their interest rates partly to defend their currencies against the dollar, partly to resolve domestic problems. In recent months they have come to view US monetary policy as an unwelcome constraint on their own policies. Their initial reaction was to urge the USA to reduce its interest rates and ease its monetary policy. In recent months, they have attempted to coordinate European interest rate policies so that their interest rate levels could be reduced together without disrupting intra-European exchange rates. They are increasingly willing to accept the consequences of a further limited weakening of their exchange rates against the dollar.

The parallel between the attitudes to exchange rates of the UK and the USA is instructive. Sterling was weak through the 1960s and in the 1970s until the end of 1976. Attempts to stem the depreciation through large-scale intervention and limited increases in interest rates failed. The authorities' conclusion was that market forces were unstoppable. When sterling's weakness was reversed, they were unwilling to act to stop sterling appreciating through 1979 and 1980 even when, by the end of 1979, they thought sterling had strengthened more than enough. This was, in part, because they were afraid that any decline they succeeded in starting would again become unstoppable. Through 1980 sterling appreciated to an extent that was recognized as damaging to UK industrial prospects, but this then came to be seen as something government was powerless to stop without endangering its restrictive monetary policy. The strength of sterling had, in addition to the oil price, the same basic cause as dollar strength — tight monetary policy justified by counter-inflationary priorities. There were two important differences. First, UK policy is traumatic only for the UK, whereas US policy not only disrupts US economic activity but also affects all other financial markets. Second, UK monetary policy was not conducted in a way that generated short-term interest rate volatility to anything like the same extent as occurred in the USA.

Successive UK governments have argued that sterling's special features have made an independent exchange rate policy for the pound inevitable. The present government's emphasis on the need for market forces to determine sterling exchange rates in response to monetary policy has been replaced by an all but explicit exchange rate target which is given great weight in the determination of monetary policy. Monetary policy is eased if it does not cause sterling to weaken. The government would like lower interest rates and a somewhat laxer monetary stance. It will follow European initiatives to reduce interest rates provided their impact on sterling is not unfavourable. UK monetary policy is discussed more fully in chapter 5.

Chapter 6 discusses options for international monetary policy over the next few years. It covers the ways in which the EMS may develop and speculates on whether it can survive in its present form. It argues that European monetary policy does need to have an explicit dollar policy but that, without US cooperation, such a policy will probably be ineffectual. Chapter 6 distinguishes between the ways in which US monetary policy is likely to change and the direction the Europeans would like to see it take. It attempts an assessment of the difference. It concludes by arguing that the US and European monetary authorities have mutual interests that probably lie just within the area of possible policy overlap, and that the gains to be had from exploring joint policy options are worthwhile for all concerned.

Finally, although this study concentrates on US monetary policy and its implications for Europe, it should be noted that the strength of the dollar has had a strong impact also on the yen and hence on Japanese competitiveness. Japanese interest rates have been directed towards domestic objectives to an even greater extent than have European interest rates, and the yen is particularly weak in consequence. It has always been a volatile currency and the sharp fluctuations in US interest rates have only reinforced its natural behaviour. Both Europe and the USA have repeatedly complained about 'excessive' Japanese competition, but the Japanese authorities can point to US monetary policy as an important cause of the extent to which the yen is undervalued, a cause, moreover, that the Japanese cannot reasonably be expected to counteract. It follows that European concern about Japanese competitiveness should be expressed in Washington rather than in Tokyo!

2 US monetary policy

It is inevitable that US policies will affect other economies, but the present nature of US monetary policy means that even short-term shifts in the stance of the Fed and the Administration are felt elsewhere almost immediately. Equally important, dollar markets have become more concerned about the short-term behaviour of the monetary aggregates than the Fed itself, and their nervousness communicates itself to foreign exchange and capital markets. This chapter discusses the reasoning underlying present US monetary philosophy, describes its development since adoption and sketches the changes it is likely to undergo. The parallels between US and UK experiences are covered in chapter 5.

In October 1979 the Federal Reserve Board, under Mr Volcker's direction, radically changed US monetary policy. Domestic monetary policy was given two associated objectives: a step reduction in the level of inflation (then running at around 13 per cent) and an end to the period of dollar weakness that had characterized the 1970s and had become particularly pronounced during the Carter Administration. The Fed announced 'tight' monetary targets (that is, the target growth rates for the monetary aggregates were well below their growth rates in the recent past, and well below the expected rate of inflation). The announcement was received with limited interest and less belief. Past precedent suggested that such targets were used only while they did not upset the objectives of the Fed and the Administration for economic activity, interest rates and the budget deficit. The Fed said that it would accept much greater interest rate volatility than in the past to ensure that the money supply grew *within* its target range. Again observers were unimpressed. Most central banks are somewhat upset if their monetary targets are exceeded but, hitherto, no monetary authority had been worried by monetary growth *below* the bottom end of its target range, which typically was accepted both as a welcome demonstration of greater than planned financial virtue and as a justification for later periods of growth in excess of the target range.

During 1980 the Fed proved that it meant what it said: the money supply grew too rapidly and short-term interest rates rose towards 20 per cent to curb it; monetary growth fell below the bottom end of the range and interest rates fell to below 10 per cent to stimulate it; monetary growth accelerated again and short-term interest rates rose sharply past their previous peak.

Within the USA these fluctuations were vigorously criticized: the first increase in interest rates was seen as an overreaction, the fall was seen as a necessary abandonment of a foolish policy and the subsequent increase was thought unsustainable.

The Fed initially justified these sharp gyrations as a necessary part of its policy, the only way of controlling the growth of the monetary aggregates within a year. Since then it has modified its position and it is now prepared to some extent to look through short-term fluctuations in monetary growth in either direction. This can be seen in its policy stance during 1981. The high short-term interest rates that prevailed until the summer ensured that the narrow money aggregate grew well below the bottom end of its target range through the second half of the year. This became clear by September but the Fed reacted by slowing the fall in interest rates, apparently on no other ground than the need to reduce interest rate volatility. The logic of this stance was followed through from December 1981, when it became clear that the growth of the monetary aggregates had again accelerated. The Fed was willing to look through the sharp upward movement in the growth of M1 (the money supply, as it is narrowly defined; *see* Glossary) to a longer-term perspective and so it constrained upward moves in interest rates.

Much of the recent rapid growth in M1 is probably a statistical artifact. Changes in US banking practice are causing individuals to switch their financial balances into bank deposits that count as part of the narrow money supply. If the Fed acts to curb this rapid growth of M1, it would be acting on the shadow rather than reality since money balances will not have really changed. This is coming to be generally accepted, but the Fed is still reluctant to change its target growth range for M1 for fear that this will be taken as a weakening of its monetary stance. Since it has emphasized the M1 target more than the M2 (money supply more widely defined) target, financial markets are concerned about the rapid growth of M1 even though they know it is a misleading indicator of what is happening in financial markets. They have a practical reason for focusing on M1: M1 figures are produced weekly while M2 figures are produced only monthly.

By the summer of 1981 money markets had learned, perhaps too well, the lessons the Fed had been teaching them since November 1979. They now look at each week's figures for the behaviour of M1 and then extrapolate a trend growth rate from them, marking interest rates up or down accordingly. The Fed, instead of acting aggressively on short-term interest rates, consistently finds itself acting to modify what it views as market over-reaction. It is ironic that the Fed is now embarrassed by the interest rate instability its own policies engendered, but the irony is not appreciated by nervous financial markets.

The Fed would like to reduce short-term interest-rate instability. Having initially placed greater emphasis on very short-term management of the monetary aggregates it would now like to encourage markets to look through even a period of two or three months' too-rapid growth of the aggregates. In recent months there has been discussion both within the Fed and in Congress of the desirability of ceasing to publish the weekly M1 figures in their present form. (They are published every Friday at 4.10 p.m. New York time and show the size of the US money supply as it is narrowly defined in the seven days up to the Wednesday of the preceding week.) These figures dominate the behaviour of US interest rates across the entire maturity spectrum.

The M1 target for 1982 is set as a range of 2.5-5.5 per cent which would permit M1 to grow during the whole of 1982 by some $20 billion. An 'up' number of $2 billion a week over the entire year would cause M1 to rise by 20-25 per cent at an annual rate. Markets tend to extrapolate the information in two or three weeks' M1 figures for the whole year. This would be foolish under any conditions, for economic variables rarely behave smoothly, but it borders on the absurd to take weekly M1 figures seriously because the authorities argue that the standard deviation of the weekly reported M1 figure (with reference to its underlying true value) is $3.5 billion. (This discrepancy is made up of both measurement error and technical factors which give a misleading short-term impression of the behaviour of the M1 series, especially given the necessarily imperfect seasonal adjustment mechanism.) There have been few occasions in recent years when M1 changes have exceeded $3.5 billion, but there have been, over the past two years, occasions when the week's 'up' or 'down' number for M1 has been sufficient to move short-term interest rates by a whole percentage point. It is interesting to reflect that financial markets can react so strongly to what is known to be, in statistical terms, a random number. Moreover, recent experience suggests that a move of this extent in short-term US interest rates can currently move the dollar against the European currencies by 2 per cent or more and can move European interest rates by a quarter per cent. Financial and foreign exchange markets are inherently uncertain, but for their movements to be controlled by such tenuous information is foolish, and a way must be found of reducing the weight that markets attach to M1.

Fed policy generated market obsession with M1 which it will eventually be able to end. Such a move, however, may require a restatement of the ground rules of US monetary policy which would, the Fed fears, weaken its credibility. It has announced (April 1982) that it intends to take steps to lessen the impact of the weekly publication of the M1 figures by publishing only a moving average of the seasonally adjusted figures, and it may delay their publication until after markets close in San Francisco on Friday evening so that market reactions to the figures will not start until after a weekend break.

The reactions of market participants to these proposals have been predictably dismissive. They will be able fairly accurately to work out the latest week's figures for themselves from what the Fed does publish. It has been suggested that it should simply stop publishing the weekly figures and publish monthly figures as the Bank of England does. There are three difficulties in introducing this:

(1)   it would require legislation since the Fed is required to publish the information under present US law;

(2)   the figures are collected on a weekly basis (unlike in the UK, where the information is collected monthly) and would probably leak to the market; and

(3) markets would react even more sharply to the monthly numbers.

The simplest way to minimize the impact of the M1 figures is for the Fed, by its actions and announcements, to make clear that it will sub-stitute its judgment of what interest rates should be for the near-mechanical rule it has been experimenting with since 1979, according to which short-term acceleration in the monetary aggregates has been met by sharp interest rate increases. This approach has been developed since mid–1981 and shows signs of being taken still further in 1982.

M1 can normally grow more slowly than nominal income because its velocity of circulation is increasing as a result of technological change. The use of credit cards, electronic transfers of funds and efficient cash management all tend to permit an increasing amount of activity to be financed with a given quantity of money. The increase in the velocity of M1 is thought likely to be of the order of 2.5 per cent a year on average. This means that any growth in nominal income at a rate faster than 8 per cent a year will require either a greater increase in the velocity of M1 or a rate of monetary growth above the target level for M1 – a range of 2.5–5.5 per cent for 1982.

If, as seems to be the case at present, the underlying rate of US inflation is of the order of 6-7 per cent a year, the M1 target is probably only compatible with little or no sustainable growth in real GDP. Any acceleration in the level of activity will, under these conditions, cause M1 to grow too rapidly, and the actions of the Fed in response would then drive interest rates sharply upwards – if market pressure had not done so already. This would then halt any growth in activity as busines-ses and individuals again sought to economize on their use of borrowed funds. The M1 target is compatible with real growth of 2-3 per cent a year only if inflation falls to around 5 per cent. While US inflation has fallen sharply, and will probably fall still further, it is unlikely to fall to that level in the near future on a sustainable basis. Thus, the present M1 target, combined with a continuing focus on its short-term behaviour, will ensure that US interest rates remain high and volatile and that activity remains steady or falls.

(Inflation in most of the major OECD economies has fallen sharply and is likely to fall further over the next year or so. The initial causes of these falls are transient factors – the world recession has driven com-modity prices, including the price of oil, down to levels that are unlikely to persist once activity picks up again. Recession has also squeezed corporate profits. Unemployment is constraining wage increases, and there is also a lagged response to the deceleration of inflation. Recorded inflation rates understate the extent of inflationary pressures, and it would be wrong to assume that inflation is going to be brought below 5 per cent in the USA on a sustainable basis unless recession is allowed to continue for longer and at a worse level than either the Administration or the Fed will countenance.)

US money markets are now also focusing on other issues than Fed policy for the narrow monetary aggregate. The Fed is contributing to this by its emphasis on a longer-term view of monetary growth — longer than a few weeks or even months. Its new emphasis on wider monetary aggregates — most notably M2 — has grown especially now that the M2 figures are, for the first time in more than a year, likely to grow within their target range.

US financial markets remain uneasy for other reasons. The immediate cause of their unease is the scale of the expected Federal government deficit. In fact the deficit, as a percentage of GNP, is reasonable by the standards of past recessions. The likely deficit for the current fiscal year — $100 billion — is equal to under 3.5 per cent of GNP. Concern is caused by projections showing the deficit rising in the next fiscal year (which begins in October 1982) and with little hope of falls thereafter. These projections of a sharply rising deficit depend in part on the prospects of a continuing US recession but are largely the consequence of President Reagan's fiscal policies. Furthermore, the so-called unified deficit, which includes state deficits and other 'off-budget' financing, now totals 6 per cent of GNP. This is large compared with the US savings ratio. Financial markets are worried that, since the US government is a good credit risk while many corporations at present are not, government competition for funds will make private borrowing either expensive or impossible.

The Administration has three objectives: first, cutting large areas of federal expenditure on transfer payments, health and education; second, raising defence expenditure sharply; and, third, cutting taxation, especially personal taxation. These three objectives are at the centre of the Administration's conservative view of the role of government; they will not be modified readily. Taken together they result in the prospect of a somewhat reflationary fiscal policy which will encounter the deflationary monetary policy implicit in the Fed's tight targets. Under these circumstances market expectations of high and volatile interest rates are understandable!

Some kind of accommodation will eventually have to be reached. It may be that the Fed will trade a limited relaxation in the monetary targets for a postponement − or at least a partial postponement − of the proposed cuts in personal taxation. Given the nature of the US political process, this sort of compromise will take some time to achieve. The commitment of the Fed to 'responsible' monetary policies is as strong as the Administration's faith in 'Reaganomics' (so-called supply side economics).

The Fed's position is stronger than might be expected partly because, constitutionally, it possesses a degree of independence of the Administration. The extent of this independence can, however, be overstated. The President could render Mr Volcker's position untenable if the Administration made clear a total lack of confidence in Fed policies. Constitutionally, Congress could direct the Fed to follow policies that Congress thought appropriate. (When reminded of this a Fed spokesman agreed that this was the position but said that Congress had never directed that monetary policies be implemented in ways that were counter to Fed views.) The reason for the Fed's strength is mainly that the Administration supports the tight monetary targets it has adopted. Administration complaints are confined to the consequent high level of interest rates which the Fed can claim is not directly within its control.

Seen against this background, the effect of European views on what US interest rates ought to be will be limited. European hopes for lower interest rates − or more stable interest rates − will have to depend on domestic US pressures for the same objectives. These pressures are strong but the conflicts in US policies that have caused high interest rates will not be quickly resolved. A feature of 1981 and the first part of 1982 was Europe's wish for lower interest rates to stimulate economic growth even at the risk of not making further progress on inflation. Until recently the USA has placed greater emphasis on reducing inflation. Now, with US inflation around 7 per cent and likely to fall somewhat further in the short term, there are signs that the Fed will focus increasingly on the need to prevent the recession worsening and so generate some recovery.

3 Links between US and European monetary policies

This chapter traces the relationships between volatile US interest rates and European monetary policies. The main transmission mechanism between the two is to be found in the US and Eurodollar markets. There are two sorts of effect: effects associated directly with interest rate volatility and those associated with the exchange rate fluctuations that are the direct consequence of interest rate movements. (The effects of high interest rates, which are also a consequence of present Fed policy, are discussed in subsequent chapters.)

The price of long-dated US bonds — say 20-year paper in the US Treasury market and ten-year paper in Euromarkets — fluctuated by 10 per cent in the two months September–October 1981. Their prices will almost certainly be both a lot higher and a lot lower during 1982 than they were at the beginning of the year. Under these circumstances investors are understandably chary of purchasing long-dated bonds. Even short-dated paper (say three years' maturity) fluctuated by 8–9 per cent in the same two-month period. In terms of capital certainty it is hardly less risky than 30-year paper because short-term interest rates fluctuate a lot more than long-term rates. Even short bonds are unattractive to risk-averse investors.

The volatility of interest rates, and hence of bond prices, has made the traditional long-term investor in bonds less willing to purchase them. The price moves described above are large enough to wipe out eight or nine months' interest earnings on the short-dated paper even at present interest levels. Under these circumstances the 'cautious' investor will prefer the capital certainty of short-term investments (that is, investments with under one year to maturity) which earn interest rates almost as high as long-term investments but without the risks. Of course bond price fluctuations offer the opportunity of capital gains (large capital gains when long-term interest rates fall sharply). By definition, the cautious investor will be willing to forgo speculative profits to avoid risking capital loss. The typical purchaser of a bond is now an institutional investor who expects to sell the bond and make capital gains in a relatively short time because he believes that after the interest fall that he anticipates rates will again rise.

Thus, bonds are long-term debt instruments which are increasingly held by professional investors with short-term objectives. This means the bond markets − and long-term interest rates − are likely to be increasingly unstable. Investment managers will buy bonds when a rally starts, and the momentum it gains will feed on itself as others seek to share in the profits. Movements in interest rates and bond prices will tend to overshoot by large amounts and then reverse, perhaps overshooting again in the opposite direction. Short-term operators have always existed in the markets. They have a worthwhile role in providing market liquidity. But short-term holders of bonds now dominate markets and make them more volatile than was the case when investors in bonds were typically matching long-term liabilities with long-term assets. Pension funds and insurance funds, the traditional long-term purchasers of bonds, have become much more concerned with short-term portfolio performance because the swings have become so much greater in interest rates and bond prices. It is sometimes argued that destabilizing speculative activity is necessarily unprofitable and that such speculators will eventually be forced out of the market. In fact, in markets in which there is no official intervention to stabilize prices (for example in Eurobond markets) speculative pressures on prices result in profits and losses among bond-holders and there is no reason why today's loser should not be tomorrow's gainer and his position over time net to balance. Markets can be unstable without any group of participants necessarily making systematic losses.

This increasing concern with short-term performance, and an aversion to bond investments, began before 1979. The acceleration in US inflation brought with it increases in interest rates and continuing capital losses on outstanding bond holdings.

If, as supporters of present Fed policy argue, the acceleration in US inflation has been broken, the peak in nominal long-term interest rates should have passed. The potential for capital gains on bonds, whose prices have fallen far below the price for which they will be redeemed when they mature, should be an added attraction. Such arguments will be treated with great scepticism by potential investors. There has now been a series of years in which investors have argued that the current percentage redemption yield to maturity is so favourable that portfolios should acquire long bonds, in the belief that interest rates must have peaked, only to find those record interest rates overtaken by a subsequent higher rate and bond prices falling in consequence.

In 1982 the combination of 15 per cent long-term interest rates and US inflation at an underlying rate of, say, 7 per cent should make bond purchases almost irresistible. It is probably the combination of price volatility with experience of increases in nominal interest rates that has resulted in real interest rates rising to unprecedented levels. One index of the impact of volatility in interest rates on markets is the need for such high real interest rates to persuade investors to hold bonds. (However, volatility is not the only reason for high real interest rates. Real rates tend to fall when inflation accelerates and rise when it slows down, probably because expectations about inflation are based on experience of the recent past. It is impossible to disentangle the two effects.)

An alternative index of the impact of interest rate volatility on investment choice is given by the price experience of floating rate notes (FRNs). An FRN is a debt instrument with a long maturity but whose capital value is largely preserved by refixing its interest rate every three or six months with reference to the short-term interest rates currently prevailing at the time of the coupon refix. The prices of such instruments prior to 1981 tended to be around 98 at the refix (the price is quoted in dollars per $100 coupon value of the FRN). During the past year prices have fluctuated but have typically tended to be 99-99½. Long-term investors, disenchanted with bond price volatility and seeking appropriate investments with lives greater than the 1-12-month life of certificates of deposit (CDs), have directed their attentions increasingly to FRNs and have pushed their prices up. The movement in prices is not dramatic compared with bond price movements (price stability is after all the attraction of 'floaters'), but it does reflect a general disenchantment with bond markets. FRN prices will probably fall back towards the levels of the 1970s if and when a sustained bond market rally takes place.

This concern with the fortunes of investment managers who acquire long-term debt instruments for the funds they manage might appear to be of limited relevance to the wider problems of managing economic activity using dollar financial markets. Long-term interest rate volatility has, however, been a factor making dollar borrowers reluctant to borrow over a long term. The US corporate treasurer who floats a long-term debt issue at 15 per cent may earn the praise of the Board and shareholders when rates rise to 16 per cent, but they will not be pleased when long rates fall a month or two later to 14 per cent. The possibility of error in the timing of long-term debt-issuing has always existed but it has become a very real risk in the 1980s. It is part of the reason for the reduction in the amount of borrowing by corporations in the domestic and Eurodollar bond markets.

A further reason for the reduction in corporate bond issues is that when bond yields are rising it becomes difficult or impossible to place new corporate paper. When a rally in bond prices is under way, that is when long-term interest rates are expected to fall, corporations tend to be reluctant to float issues until the rally is largely over and the cost of funding is lower. Timing debt-issues so that willing debt-issuers can find ready purchasers becomes hard in volatile markets!

Large numbers of corporate borrowers want to issue new medium- and long-term corporate debt in domestic and Eurodollar financial markets. They would welcome the opportunity of having a much greater element of certainty in their financial planning before embarking on further investment or, in many cases, simply of ensuring their survival in the present US recession. The structure of corporate debt in the USA is now more short-term and unfavourable than at any time in the postwar period.

UK companies, accustomed to using short-term finance on a long-term basis, might have little sympathy for this predicament. Corporate debt structure, however, plays a part in determining the scale of US investment and the falls in investment play their part in driving the USA deeper into recession. Furthermore, a recovery in the world economy would be greatly helped by a resumption of US growth.

US interest rate volatility is echoed in European money markets, but the repercussions are generally muted. When US interest rates increase, there is a tendency for European rates to harden, but a 1 per cent increase in US rates may bring increases of only $\frac{1}{8}-\frac{1}{4}$ per cent in Deutschmark rates. It is the high average level of US interest rates that has a major impact on European rates. German interest rates would probably have been 2–3 percentage points lower in 1981 and the first half of 1982 if they were driven only by domestic considerations.

Short-term movements in US interest rates do have an immediate impact on Europe. A rise in dollar short-term rates causes dollar exchange rates against the European currencies to strengthen. The reasons for this close positive interrelationship between movements in short-term interest rates and exchange rates are worth examining since it is largely a phenomenon of the past three years and is particularly marked in exchange rates against the dollar.

Day-to-day interest rate movements do not necessarily influence exchange rates in a predictable direction. The normal reason for sharp increases in interest rates is a belated attempt by a country's monetary authority to stave off speculative attack on the exchange rate. France, Belgium and the Irish Republic offer recent examples of this. Most countries prefer to maintain low interest rates to foster activity and raise them only when domestic inflationary pressures or external constraints oblige them to do so. US interest rates, however, can rise sharply from one week to another or from one day to another, for reasons which, to outside observers, seem unimportant.

Banks making markets in foreign exchange will generally seek broadly balanced books, but if they find that the US interest rate for overnight deposits has gone up sharply they will leave their dollar positions open both because the overnight cost of borrowing dollars has risen and because they will expect the dollar to strengthen.

In some money markets – indeed in most markets – the overnight rate does not necessarily influence rates out to three months or a year. In the USA at present, however, a high overnight 'Federal funds' rate can be taken by markets as an indication of a tightening of the Fed's stance and can shift upwards the whole yield curve – that is, interest rates for all lengths of maturity. If, say, the three-months Eurodollar rate rises while the three-months Deutschmark rate is unchanged, then the cost of forward cover on the mark rises, and companies will be more reluctant to buy Deutschmarks forward (that is, to sell dollars forward). These companies will either postpone taking out cover or leave their dollar sales for execution later in the spot market. This will tend to strengthen the dollar.

Downward moves in short-term US interest rates will have the opposite effect by moving the balance of advantage in favour of the Deutschmark. Fluctuations in interest rates are directly transmitted into fluctuations in exchange rates.

Does this sort of exchange rate volatility matter? Experience with companies dealing in foreign markets seems to suggest that it does not matter very much. It appears to do little to dissuade them from using those markets, and in many, or even most, cases it appears to have little immediate impact on the prices they set. This is surprising. A move of 2-3 per cent in an exchange rate ought to translate into a move several times larger in the profits on any particular transaction, given that companies typically do not pass short-term exchange rate fluctuations on to customers so that the gains and losses on the whole transaction are loaded on to profits. Companies view this uncertainty as part of the costs of foreign trade and tend to take a philosophical view of the fact that exchange rates may fluctuate through a range of some 1-3 per cent in a week.

The attitude of companies to foreign currency risks and treatment of them are described in the Appendix. This can be summarized as showing that an awareness of the need for management of foreign currency exposure has grown sharply in the period since the breakdown of the Bretton Woods system and that in almost all companies engaged in foreign trade a large part of the time of the finance or treasury department is now devoted to foreign exchange matters. Seen against overall company costs, however, the resources spent on this are insignificant. Moreover, these departments are concerned with insulating their companies against large foreign exchange moves as much as against short-term volatility. Increased short-term foreign exchange rate volatility has had little effect on company behaviour. Any kind of additional price uncertainty ought to increase the profit margins sought on foreign trade or to reduce companies' willingness to engage in it, but it is difficult to find cases to demonstrate this.

4 The European Community and the dollar

The EMS was created in the same year that the Fed adopted its restrictive monetary stance. The two events were, indirectly, connected, for both were responses to the weakness of the dollar in foreign exchange markets. The EMS might have been expected to provide a suitable institutional framework for developing European responses to the problems posed by the USA's high and volatile interest rates. It has in fact played little part in focusing the attention of European monetary authorities on outside problems. They have generally directed their energies to managing their exchange rates against the Deutschmark and left their dollar exchange rates effectively under Bundesbank control (a situation the Bundesbank has welcomed). Not until 1981 did the member states of the European Community discuss the constraints Fed policy imposed on their action and begin to consider ways of limiting the unwelcome effects of that policy. Criticism of US monetary policy remains surprisingly muted, given the scale of its impact on European monetary management. The reasons for the EMS's inward-looking orientation are, in part, to be found in the history of European Community exchange rate arrangements, which began a decade ago with the 'snake in the tunnel'.

The snake arrangements were set up in 1972 after the intervention limits of all currencies against the dollar were widened to plus or minus $2\frac{1}{4}$ per cent (under the Smithsonian Agreement, December 1971). This meant that any currency could fluctuate against the dollar within a $4\frac{1}{2}$ per cent band. It also meant that, for example, the French franc could fluctuate against the Deutschmark within a 9 per cent band because each had its rates fixed not against the other but against the dollar. (Suppose the franc is strong and the Deutschmark weak, then the franc will be at its upper intervention limit against the dollar, the Deutschmark at its lower intervention limit. Now suppose the franc weakens and the Deutschmark strengthens; the franc depreciates $4\frac{1}{2}$ per cent against the dollar, the Deutschmark strengthens $4\frac{1}{2}$ per cent against the dollar and the Deutschmark strengthens by 9 per cent against the franc.)

In the European Community this was seen as disruptive on two counts: it would penalize intra-European trade and favour trade with the USA and the wide range would permit member states of the Community to follow 'divergent economic policies' because they would be subject to only a lax exchange rate constraint. The concept of 'divergent economic policies' and the belief that fixed exchange rates within the snake or the EMS could promote 'convergence' has been one of the main features of Community thinking on European monetary policy. To preserve fixed exchange rates, weak currency member states would be obliged to tighten monetary policy and raise interest rates. The deflationary impact of these measures would reduce their inflation rates and, eventually, improve their competitive positions. They would be able to reduce interest rates once they had achieved this adjustment. The German authorities have normally been the chief proponents of this view because in general it placed the burden of adjustment on the other members of the EMS. Other member states, with the exception of France under President Giscard d'Estaing, have been less enthusiastic about the need for 'convergence'.

The snake in the tunnel restricted member states' currencies to fluctuations within a $2\frac{1}{4}$ per cent band against each other: half the size of their maximum permitted fluctuation against the dollar. It was possible for this spread to occur with all currencies strong against the dollar (with the strongest snake currency pressing against its upper intervention limit with the dollar) or with all currencies weak against the dollar (with the weakest snake currency pressing against its lower intervention limit with the dollar). The dollar intervention limits set an absolute upper and lower limit for member currency fluctuations – the 'tunnel'. Member currencies moved within their narrower agreed band against each other while strengthening or weakening together against the dollar; hence, they wriggled up and down – the snake in the tunnel.

The snake in the tunnel was a creature of the early 1970s. When the dollar began to float, currencies lost the intervention limits that had structured foreign exchange markets through the postwar period, and the tunnel ended. The snake continued but there was no institutional framework empowering the Community to act to influence their exchange rates against the dollar. Member states in effect pegged their currencies against the Deutschmark and the Bundesbank sought to guide the dollar-Deutschmark exchange rate, as is now the case with the EMS. (This has never been the legal or formal position. In the EMS, for example, all exchange rates are given against the European Currency Unit (ECU), which is the artificial currency created by the Community. In practice EMS exchange rates are pegged to the Deutschmark.) Sterling came under pressure almost immediately because of its own particular problems and left the snake rather than devalue and run the risk of further speculative attack. The strength of the Deutschmark rapidly placed the snake under strain, and Italy and France had to abandon it. France rejoined for a brief period a few years later but again decided to leave rather than devalue, underlining in doing so how difficult any exchange rate agreement with the Deutschmark bloc would be.

The important features of the snake were:

(1) it was developed against the background of the fixed exchange rate system;

(2) it was disrupted promptly by speculative attacks on the weaker currencies within it, though it survived in a limited form with the continuing membership of Belgium, the Netherlands, Luxembourg, Denmark and with the associated membership of Norway and Sweden;

(3) it contained no provision for joint European initiatives to manage the snake exchange rates against the dollar;

(4) its intention was to oblige member states of the Community to harmonize their economic policies through the discipline of fixed exchange rates and, moveover initially to promote European Monetary Union by progressively narrowing the band within which member currencies could move.

The EMS is the snake brought back to life. The reasons for the comparative longevity of the EMS have, as is argued below, little to do with the EMS itself.

The genesis of the EMS is fascinating for students of politics: it appears to have been the outcome of an informal discussion between President Giscard d'Estaing and Chancellor Schmidt in 1978. They subsequently informed a surprised press conference, and their own equally astonished officials, that they thought that the European Community should again seek to achieve monetary union. Thus, two heads of state, unbriefed by their own political advisers or officials, made an agreement in principle on a concept they then left to be articulated over the following months both by their own administrations and by the governments of other member states. It is, none the less, possible to overstate the extent to which the EMS was the result of a personal initiative by two heads of state, since the European Commission had been arguing for a revived snake for some time, and this had earlier been the subject of a speech by Roy Jenkins as President of the Commission.

The EMS was a Franco–German political creation, but during 1978 politicians and officials in all the then nine member states of the Community struggled to make economic and administrative sense of a *fait accompli*. It is noteworthy that French and German negotiators were frequently as confused as anyone else about what they were hoping to achieve.

All nine member states, including the UK, joined the EMS. The UK, however, decided it would not participate in the exchange rate provisions of the EMS. (The name 'EMS' is and was used also to denote the exchange rate provisions of the system. It is used in the rest of this paper in this, its conventional, sense.) Although UK membership of the system has some practical impact on the EMS – for example, sterling forms part of the European Currency Unit (ECU) – in effect the British government said it would not join what it saw as a new 'snake' but would demonstrate its pro-European stance by joining the overall arrangements of the system. This was, rightly, widely regarded as meaningless, since in what was intended to be the first stage of EMS development the exchange rate provisions are all that matters. Formally, the UK has never refused outright to implement the exchange rate arrangements, but has not yet found the moment right (*see* chapter 5).

This description of the origins of the EMS has yet to mention its relationship with the dollar because it was only partly a response to pressures from across the Atlantic. It was, and is, intended to be a mechanism for achieving the eventual economic convergence of member states of the Community on the road towards full economic union.

The EMS was set up in a period when continuing dollar weakness was taken as given. The dollar's days as the world's predominant, almost sole, reserve currency were thought to be numbered, rather as sterling's role had been weakened more than a decade earlier. In that sense the ECU was a response to a problem posed by US policies. It was an attempt to create a European version of the SDR — a European reserve asset that could be held by monetary authorities unwilling to hold depreciating dollars, or indeed SDRs that have the dollar as their largest single component. The German authorities saw the development of a reserve role for the Deutschmark as potentially disastrous since disruptive capital account flows already occurred frequently on a scale unwelcome to them. If a substitute were needed for the dollar, they argued, at least let the burden of providing a reserve asset be a European one rather than solely a German one. The period of dollar strength that began at the end of 1979 has consigned reserve asset diversification so far down the list of international monetary priorities that it is almost forgotten. It is an issue that will emerge again when the present extraordinary strength of the dollar ends, but until then policy-makers have other problems to resolve.

The EMS has survived as long as it has largely because of the dollar's strength. 'Speculative inflows' of funds into the Deutschmark and Dutch guilder were regular features of the international monetary scene during the 1970s. The strength of the dollar since the end of 1979 has removed the potentially most disruptive force from European financial markets. Indeed the Deutschmark became so weak against the dollar during the winter of 1980 that it fell to the bottom of the EMS and for a period there were suggestions that it would have to devalue. There are some sources of weakness of the Deutschmark peculiar to Germany itself (most notably the impact of the oil price shock on its balance of payments and the Polish crisis), but the strength of the dollar not only attracted funds that might otherwise have gone to Germany but also caused capital outflows from Deutschmark financial markets. The factors which made the Deutschmark strong in the 1970s — low inflation, soundly based export growth, a well-run economy and conservative monetary policies — all remain. The Deutschmark has been tamed

29

within the EMS only because of its weakness against the dollar. This was demonstrated in October 1981 when, during what was to be a temporary period of limited dollar weakness, the strength of the Deutschmark was sufficient to force an EMS realignment.

The case for the view that fixed but adjustable exchange rates lead to economic convergence is a poor one. It is probably true that an irrevocably fixed exchange rate will oblige two countries to follow compatible monetary policies. (Under the monetary union between the UK and the Republic of Ireland, which dated from early in the nineteenth century and was ended when the UK decided not to participate in the EMS exchange rate provisions, Ireland was obliged to share in all sterling's fortunes and to adapt its policies accordingly.) But the reality of the EMS is that exchange rates are adjustable and that countries can follow divergent economic policies within it.

The Belgian devaluation within the EMS – effectively an 8.5 per cent realignment against the Deutschmark in February 1982 – showed that in the end exchange rates give way rather than economic policies, and that a period of many years of virtual exchange rate stability against the Deutschmark had not brought about sustainable economic 'convergence'. Incidentally, the Belgian devaluation came close to ending a long-standing currency union: the Luxembourg franc has no separate existence from the Belgian franc, but the Duchy was not consulted about the devaluation, would have opposed it and will, it claims, separate the Luxembourg franc from the Belgian should the Belgian authorities seek a further realignment.

The EMS is not in sufficiently good health to be able to undertake major initiatives with respect to the dollar. The Belgians reportedly wished to devalue by 12 per cent within the EMS. Other member states argued that the devaluation should be half this size and Belgium threatened to leave the EMS. The Belgian franc remains within the EMS but is already subject to further speculative attack.

The French have always chosen to support Community exchange rate initiatives until prevented by 'market pressures' from doing so. President Mitterrand's government has, however, chosen to conduct economic policies in a way which ensures further divergence of French and German economic performances and is already bringing the franc under speculative attack. If high French interest rates become the price for franc stability in the EMS, then that price will be seen as too high and a further devaluation accepted. Thereafter the French government will have two choices: to continue present policies until the frequency and scale of French realignments within EMS become unacceptable to other member states; or to accept that fiscal reflation will be sustainable in conjunction with relative exchange rate stability only if French interest rates are allowed to rise sharply. The French horror of a return to their postwar experiences of inflation and exchange rate instability may yet lead to a change in government policies which will permit continued French membership of the EMS, but there is no sign of such a change. If policies do not change, the franc will have to leave the EMS.

The wider objectives of the EMS have been abandoned. Attempts to celebrate its third anniversary by widening its scope ran rapidly into opposition, most notably from the Bundesbank. The Bundesbank opposed the setting up of the EMS in 1979 and now fears that attempts to extend EMS objectives will oblige it to act in ways that would generate inflationary pressures within Germany.

The proposal for the reform of the EMS that received most attention was that an attempt should be made to stabilize EMS currencies against the dollar. This was to be achieved as far as possible through an accord with the US monetary authorities on US interest rates, but where that failed EMS member states were to use intervention (rather than countervailing interest rate policy) to support their currencies. In the context of a strong dollar it is natural that emphasis should be placed on intervention to support European currencies and on the need to curb US interest rates.

Bundesbank opposition to these proposals has been firm and well publicized. There appears to be a fear that German foreign exchange reserves would be committed to propping up not only the Deutschmark but also weaker European currencies. If Germany adopted an explicit exchange rate target for the Deutschmark, then that target, combined with existing EMS provisions, would have precisely the result feared. EMS targets for exchange rates against the dollar would reduce German flexibility on its exchange rate management. So far the German authorities have always given way to pressures on the Deutschmark and have intervened only when limited action looked likely to have significant results.

31

The EMS is too weak for a dollar exchange rate objective to be feasible. In France, Belgium and the Irish Republic governments are unwilling to follow the monetary and fiscal policies that might enable them to defend their present exchange rates within the EMS. In Germany, Bundesbank concern about the potentially inflationary effects of the EMS was never resolved. The UK now sees its perspective on the EMS vindicated: the EMS was the snake in fancy dress and likely to fail. Under these circumstances the EMS will carry no conviction if it seeks to widen the scope of its actions to cover the dollar.

It will be unfortunate if the EMS does break up again. 'Convergence' was never feasible as a result of exchange rate rules, and it is noteworthy that the UK outside the EMS has brought its economic policies and performance much closer to those of Germany than have France, Belgium, Italy or Ireland within. The most sensible case that can be made for the EMS is that it establishes a zone of exchange rate stability in a world of otherwise unstable exchange rates. There are costs involved in trade when prices are uncertain because of volatile exchange rates, and the EMS could continue to offer a way of reducing such costs.

The EMS is unlikely to offer a convincing mechanism for dealing with the problems US monetary policy poses for Europe because exchange rate rules and coordinated European intervention would lack credibility. There has, however, been a general change of attitude in Europe, and the European monetary authorites have begun to develop coordinated responses. In the second half of 1981 the falls in US interest rates were used as an opportunity to strengthen the European currencies by leaving European interest rates unchanged and allowing interest rate differentials to narrow. In the first quarter of 1982 the European authorities brought down interest rates in a concerted attempt to ease European monetary policy in the face of what they viewed as an unduly tight US monetary stance. The next time US interest rates fall, the member states of the Community will seek to cut their own interest rates and further ease their monetary policies.

Unwillingness to see their currencies weaken any further against the dollar has so far explained the Europeans' reluctance to lower interest rates. Faced with their domestic recessions and the world recession they all want interest rates several percentage points lower. They appear to take the view that further limited and concerted cuts in interest rates would be a persuasive demonstration of their point that US interest rates are too high for the health of either the US or the world economies since it would bring their exchange rates under further pressure and leave the dollar still more overvalued.

The need to stop an even further weakening of the Deutschmark against the dollar explains why short-term German interest rates are 9 per cent (June 1982) rather than the 6-7 per cent the Bundesbank probably views as desirable, given present domestic inflation and the extent of the German recession. It might be assumed that the German authorities would welcome an exchange rate against the dollar of, say, DM2.40 or even weaker, for it makes German exports very competitive compared with US exports. In fact they would welcome an exchange rate some 10-15 per cent stronger because of the beneficial effect it would have on inflation. (It is less certain that other European states would welcome the Deutschmark strengthening to this extent since a further EMS realignment would then be inevitable.)

There is probably little more that the European monetary authorities can do. They already attempt to stabilize their exchange rates against the dollar, but such action is fruitless when US interest rates remain volatile and the USA, as a matter of principle, refuses to undertake intervention in foreign exchange markets. US money market management must be a US domestic concern. All that European governments can do is describe the problems that present US polices cause for them and hope that these will be taken account of in future changes in those policies.

5 UK monetary policy

UK monetary policy has changed in the course of the early 1980s. The emphasis on monetary targets and monetary policy reaching back to 1976 was narrowed sharply during the first year of office of the Conservative government (1979-80) to an all but exclusive focus on slowing the growth of sterling M3 (money supply; *see* Glossary); the government has since evolved a wider set of objectives covering the general monetary management of the economy. At any one time a particular objective will predominate. At present, the UK, in common with the rest of the European Community, wishes to foster economic recovery by lowering interest rates and generally easing monetary policy. This objective is subject to a range of constraints, most notably the need to ensure that inflation continues to decelerate. As a result, the extent to which interest rates can be lowered is limited by an exchange rate objective, since a weak pound would generate inflationary pressures in spite of the depth of current recession.

This harnessing of interest rates to an exchange rate policy will probably result in UK monetary policy being linked to that of the USA in the remainder of the 1980s in a way that did not occur during the 1970s (nor indeed in 1980 and the first half of 1981). That said, the nature of the UK exchange rate objective mutes US influences, since the UK monetary authorities focus not on the exchange rate against the dollar but on the 'effective exchange rate'. This is a trade-weighted basket of the currencies of the UK's major trading partners, expressed as an index number with 1975 = 100 as the base. To the limited extent that the rest of the European Community succeeds in distancing itself from the pressures of dollar money markets, so too can the UK (and there is a feedback effect from lower sterling interest rates to the potential for lower European interest rates).

UK policy towards Europe and the USA has always been Janus-like in trade, foreign policy and economic policy, as well as culturally. In European eyes, the UK has looked too much across the Atlantic. The one brief period when the UK joined the snake in 1972 was when all European exchange rates were still pegged to the dollar in the last months of the general fixed exchange rate regime. In fact the UK left the snake before the fixed exchange rate regime itself broke up not because any potential conflict of interest between dollar and Deutschmark exchange rate targets had become apparent but because sterling was suffering from one of its recurring bouts of weakness.

Thereafter during the 1970s, sterling's exchange rate objective was generally given either in terms of the dollar or in terms of the effective exchange rate. Between 1974 and 1977 the Labour government had an explicit exchange rate target of 'maintaining the competitive position of sterling', which was taken to mean that sterling should weaken each year sufficiently to compensate for the difference between UK inflation and inflation in competing countries. During this period the dollar weakened against the Deutschmark to an extent that broadly reflected the US and German inflation differential, and so a dollar exchange rate target for sterling was roughly consistent with a broader objective of competitiveness.

Once sterling had recovered from its November 1976 crisis, with the help of policy measures from the International Monetary Fund (IMF) and a more restrictive monetary stance, a sterling–dollar target was in effect adopted for the following seven or eight months. The authorities maintained that the competitive position of sterling would be their chief concern in exchange rate management and they intervened to stop sterling appreciating until September 1977. The restrictiveness of domestic monetary policy then began to attract capital inflows. These were seen as endangering the monetary target and so the exchange rate objective for sterling was eventually abandoned. While some of the debate on exchange rate policy was carried on in terms of an effective exchange rate target, sterling fluctuated against the Deutschmark within a 7 per cent band in the first half of 1977 and moved within only a $\frac{1}{2}$ per cent band against the dollar. By October 1977 the period of sterling strength, which was to end three years later, in November 1980, had begun. During this period there was no exchange rate target for sterling since the authorities directed monetary policy to domestic objectives without regard for exchange rate consequences. The change in the dollar's behaviour since the end of 1979 made the distinction between a dollar exchange rate target and an effective exchange rate target more important, but the distinction only became relevant when, during 1981, the authorities again accepted that they should try to influence the exchange rate.

To talk of exchange rate targets in the context of the UK in the 1980s is somewhat misleading. The Conservative government has, since it took office in May 1979, denied having an exchange rate target. 'Market forces', it is argued, are irresistible because of the scale of flows of international funds. This approach has considerable appeal to the monetary authorities. They still remember sterling's apparently 'unstoppable' collapse to US $1.56 in October 1976. Their impotence then in the face of international capital flows was used to justify their inaction in the face of an almost equally 'unstoppable' rise to US $2.47 in October 1980. If monetary policy is given a domestic objective and directed to the pursuit of that objective regardless of external developments, then capital flows will be on a scale that makes exchange rate movements 'unstoppable' by intervention and the exhortations of the authorities. In the 1970s an exchange rate objective required directing interest rate policy primarily to that objective, and this is even more the case in the 1980s.

The UK authorities continue to claim that they have no exchange rate objective for sterling. This is true in the sense that an effective exchange rate target implies no particular rate for the pound against the dollar or Deutschmark. It may even be true in the sense that an effective exchange rate of 88 or 89 is seen as no more or less desirable than an effective exchange rate of 92 or 93. That said, the authorities have shown their willingness to stop the exchange rate falling too far by raising interest rates by four percentage points in September 1981 and by cutting interest rates only when this does not adversely affect the currency.

In the March 1982 budget the Chancellor of the Exchequer Sir Geoffrey Howe announced that the sterling M3 target, which, formally at least, had been the monetary target guiding policy since 1976, would be replaced by a wider set of targets covering the whole range of monetary aggregates and that monetary policy would take account of other economic factors. (It is generally believed that the Bank of England would have liked an explicit public commitment to a target range for the effective exchange rate since this had been government policy for a year or so. The Chancellor's refusal to make such a pledge was presumably based on the view that it would do nothing to improve market behaviour and could prove burdensome if the government were overtaken by events.) This change of emphasis is widely believed to mark the end of a commitment to deflationary monetary policy in the UK, but while US and German monetary policies remain restrictive an effective exchange rate target for sterling still implies a fairly tight UK monetary stance.

It could be said that the effective exchange rate objective for sterling means that UK monetary policy is, like German policy, the prisoner of high US interest rates. This view can be overstated. In 1982, UK inflation has an underlying rate of just under 10 per cent, the monetary aggregates are growing at about 12-14 per cent and output may grow by around 2 per cent. Under these circumstances the scope for sustainable cuts in interest rates is limited to reductions of perhaps one or two percentage points.

Present UK concern with high US interest rates starts from a different perspective. First, it is believed that a recovery in world activity waits on US developments. Second, a stronger sterling–dollar exchange rate together with a weaker sterling–Deutschmark exchange rate would be much more attractive for the UK because it would improve competitiveness with respect to Europe without adding greatly to inflationary pressures (the effect of sterling weakening against EMS currencies would generate some inflationary pressures but these would be offset in part by sterling strengthening against the dollar). This requires a weakening of the dollar which will occur only when US interest rates fall.

As chapter 4 described, the UK formally joined the EMS in 1979 but did not associate itself with the exchange rate arrangements. This decision was a difficult one at the time because EMS objectives of convergent economic policies and eventual European Monetary Union were taken seriously in London. There was a widespread belief that the EMS would continue to develop into more than the snake and that a 'two-tier' Community would grow up. By not accepting the exchange rate provisions of the EMS the UK apparently ran the risk of condemning itself to a quasi-associated-member status in the Community. Given the difficulties the EMS is now experiencing and the lack of political will in Germany and France to see it develop further, these worries now seem exaggerated or baseless. They did not seem so in 1979, and the Bank of England devoted a great deal of effort to drawing up a workable institutional framework for the EMS and for its artificial currency, the ECU.

The UK did not at the time accept the exchange rate provision of the EMS because it was thought that sterling would be dragged up by the Deutschmark to unsustainable levels against the dollar. An additional consideration was that sterling would suffer yet another bout of foreign exchange market weakness and the then government would face the embarassment of having to abandon the EMS with the maximum amount of unfavourable publicity in the run-up to a general election. It is ironic that if sterling had pegged its exchange rate to the Deutschmark in March 1979 it would have stood lower against the Deutschmark than was in fact the case in every subsequent month except the four-month period beginning in October 1979 (when the Deutschmark strengthened by a maximum of 4-5 per cent against the pound). This point can be illustrated in another way: if sterling had been pegged to the Deutschmark when EMS exchange rate arrangements became operative, sterling would never have strengthened beyond US $2.20, whereas in fact it was above this level for virtually the whole of 1980 and the first quarter of 1981, reaching $2.47 in the last quarter of 1980.

The effects of this on the UK economy would have been mixed. To keep sterling within the EMS it would have been necessary to lower considerably the average level of UK interest rates throughout the period from the inception of the exchange rate arrangements. It is almost certain that industrial output would then have been much higher, unemployment lower (but probably still well above two million) and inflation would have remained firmly in double-digit numbers, say 12-14 per cent. It was incorrect to say 'there is no alternative': the monetary authorities could have directed policy towards keeping sterling within the EMS, indeed could have done so much less painfully than they expected. Mrs Thatcher's government did not welcome the continued strengthening of sterling through 1980, and it is clear that much of that strength could have been avoided by a temporary relaxation of its monetary stance.

This said, the drastic loss of competitiveness of sterling over the past few years may be helping to bring about a necessary restructuring of UK industry and a sustainable single-digit inflation. Paradoxically, an attempt to avoid the discipline of convergence to German economic patterns brought about much more rigorous deflationary policies than the Conservative government initially envisaged and may, if those policies are sustained, yet bring about a break in the inflationary spiral.

The reasons why the UK would not now adhere to the exchange rate provisions of the EMS are as follows.

(1)   The EMS survives as a Deutschmark bloc. The addition of sterling would add to disruptive pressures within the EMS, given sterling's large role in international financial markets.

(2)   The experiences of 1976 and 1980 show how sterling can develop an 'unstoppable' momentum, first in one direction and then in the opposite direction, in which circumstances it would probably not be within the power of the UK monetary authorities to remain within the EMS.

(3)   Sterling is overvalued against EMS currencies and to join the EMS now would lock sterling in at an uncompetitive exchange rate. The authorities would not be willing to see sterling depreciate against the Deutschmark unless it could maintain something like its existing exchange rate against the dollar and so limit the inflationary impact of the depreciation. This view means the UK authorities have in effect a dollar–Deutschmark exchange rate objective.

(4)   UK trade patterns make some sort of stability against the dollar as desirable as stability against the Deutschmark since, in addition to its trade with the USA, much UK third country trade is dollar-denominated.

(5)   Sterling is the only 'oil currency' of the European Community. Movements in the price of oil have opposite effects on the UK's current account and on the current accounts of other member states, which could add to disruptive pressures within the EMS.

(6)   The EMS has fulfilled only one of its initial objectives: it has

created a zone of limited exchange rate stability. It is now as likely to break up as to develop further along its initially intended path to monetary union.

Advocates of UK adherence to EMS exchange rate arrangements advance the following counter-arguments.

(1) All existing members of the EMS exchange rate arrangements would welcome UK membership precisely because it would transform the present snake into something wider than a Deutschmark bloc. Even the German authorities believe UK membership would add a useful new dimension to the EMS. The smaller member states all want a counterweight to the Deutschmark both for political reasons and because sterling might limit the extent to which they are dragged up by the Deutschmark in periods when it strengthens sharply.

(2) The Bank of England's experience with exchange rate management shows that an interest rate policy directed primarily towards an exchange rate target would be effective. This means that interest rate policy would sometimes be used in ways that conflict with domestic objectives, but that is in any event already happening.

(3) The fact that sterling is overvalued against EMS currencies is a problem. It is not, however, a permanent one, for there will come a time, probably within the next year or so, when the sterling–Deutschmark rate will be at a level that would be generally acceptable by a criterion of competitiveness. (This would happen if the dollar weakens somewhat as US interest rates fall.) The present thrust of official thinking would deny that this would be an appropriate time to join the exchange rate arrangements since even then there would be no certainty that the dollar would remain weak against the EMS.

(4) The structure of UK trade patterns, and more particularly their currency denomination, is not a good justification for the continuing emphasis on the effective exchange rate. While it is true that a somewhat larger proportion of UK exports go to dollar-oriented markets than is the case with other members of the Community (where intra-Community trade is more important), the UK overall trade position is less sensitive to dollar fluctuations than theirs because other member states are large oil importers and oil is dollar-denominated. Moreover, the UK's prospects for growth in Community export markets are more favourable than any other member's, and exchange rate stability may

be helpful in developing those export markets.

(5)   The fact that sterling is a 'petro-currency' should not be taken in isolation. As the preceding paragraph argues, it lessens the sensitivity of the trade balance to dollar fluctuations and enables sterling better to maintain stable exchange rates against EMS currencies. More important, the sensitivity of capital markets to interest rate fluctuations means that the authorities have a powerful tool for offsetting even large fluctuations in trade account prospects caused by changes in the price of oil.

(6)   Although the most compelling reason for full membership of the EMS has receded (there is little immediate prospect of the EMS evolving into anything more than a snake), this does not mean that the EMS will never evolve further. The history of the Community is of a series of political initiatives which push its development less far than the idealists want but further than the cynics think possible. UK support might prove important in encouraging the next stage of the EMS development.

(7)   In an era of exchange rate volatility the EMS offers a zone where a return to something like the Bretton Woods system of fixed but adjustable pegged exchange rates is possible. That is still a worthwhile gain, even given current European disenchantment with developing the EMS further and the prospect of more frequent EMS realignments. Furthermore, the next development in the EMS should be its extension to include some arrangements for a dollar policy. Such a development would be more likely with UK participation than without it but would still need US support before it could be effective.

6 European initiatives

Earlier chapters have described European responses to the USA's changed policy stance. The European economies have had to absorb the impact of a shift from a lax to a tight US monetary policy. In the next few years they will have to continue to adapt to the changed ground rules for international money markets that have resulted. Further shifts in the stance of US policy will inevitably occur and require additional adjustments in European policies. Separately, European economies can only respond to such shifts; acting together they could take initiatives of their own. The cost of adjustment to sudden changes in US policies is high; if member states of the European Community could identify common interests which justified joint action they would be able to exert a greater influence on the direction of international monetary policy.

European initiatives can be made either in a Community context, most readily through the EMS, or through specific initiatives on particular issues. The most noteworthy example of the latter was the agreement to lower interest rates jointly at the beginning of 1982.

Ideally, a European accord on international monetary policy would have the following elements:

(1)   a system of fixed but adjustable exchange rates for all the major European currencies, including sterling, against each other;

(2)   a compatible set of exchange rate targets against the US dollar;

(3)   agreement on interest rates consistent with both (1) and (2); and

(4)   a definition of the extent to which foreign exchange intervention can be used to fix (1) and (2).

The European monetary authorities would welcome the cooperation of the US authorities in four ways:

(1)   US willingness to use direct intervention to reduce short-term exchange rate fluctuations (i.e. 'smoothing');

(2)   reduced US interest rate volatility;

(3)   a lower level for US interest rates but one still higher than inflation; and

(4)   a stable US monetary stance: a commitment not to change policies in ways that will again bring about a weak dollar and too low interest rates.

By the standards of most proposals for international monetary reform this is a modest set of requirements. It requires no secession of national sovereignty and comparatively limited changes in existing policies. This notwithstanding, prospects for its realization in the next few years are poor.

The elements of a possible European accord can be amplified point by point, as follows.

(1)   The UK is reluctant to make explicit its exchange rate target, and to switch from an effective exchange rate target to, in effect, a target against the Deutschmark, especially while the government considers sterling overvalued against the Deutschmark. The authorities have become more openly committed to an effective exchange rate target for sterling. They may yet feel able to accept the exchange rate provisions of the EMS should the Deutschmark be able to stabilize itself against the dollar at a level that permits sterling to appreciate somewhat against the dollar while weakening against the Deutschmark. (Exchange rate targets have a habit of being overtaken by events but the sorts of numbers the UK authorities would probably wish to see are $/£1.90, DM/$2.00 and DM/£3.80 compared with current rates (June 1982) of roughly $/£1.80, DM/$2.40 and DM/£4.30.)

(2)   Recent proposals for stabilizing EMS exchange rates against the dollar have foundered in the face of German opposition. At present EMS rates are in effect pegged against the Deutschmark and the Bundesbank then manages the dollar-Deutschmark rate. Any attempt to introduce mechanisms for overall European management of EMS currencies against the dollar would necessarily limit the Bundesbank's flexibility in deciding its own policies with respect to the dollar. Without

political support for European initiatives within Germany, the Bundesbank will not accept the constraints on its actions that would result from any widening of EMS objectives in exchange rate stabilization. Chancellor Schmidt's weak position in domestic politics means that the Federal government is less willing to take the strong line on the EMS that it felt able to follow at the time of its creation. This obstacle to change, while a weighty one, is not immovable. Were sterling to join the exchange rate arrangements of the EMS, an explicit dollar policy would become almost inevitable, and the potential entry of sterling has been welcomed by other EMS members precisely because a counterbalance to the Deutschmark would then exist.

(3) The relationships among EMS interest rates are imposed by market forces, and their absolute levels are in effect determined by German rates. As chapter 3 argued, given the potential scale of international capital flows, only interest rate movements can make exchange rate targets viable. Accord among European countries on the level of their exchange rates against the dollar would then determine the general level of their interest rates, unless the decision continues to be left to the Bundesbank.

(4) Intervention can be of two sorts: either for the day-to-day smoothing of exchange rate fluctuations or, on a large scale, over a period of weeks or months, as an alternative to interest rate movements. The scope for the latter is increasingly recognized as limited, not least because Eurocurrency markets are so much larger than any country's official reserves.

Turning next to what the Europeans might ask of the USA, it is worth noting that these points are largely independent of the European issues described above in that they can be regarded as measures to improve international financial stability regardless of European action.

(1) The US authorities' refusal to intervene directly in foreign exchange markets except under exceptional circumstances must have contributed to day-to-day exchange rate volatility. It would be possible for the USA to undertake smoothing operations subject to a requirement that net changes in reserves over, say, a one- to three-month period be negligible. Present US policy on intervention, from a European perspective, is irresponsible: the major participant in world financial markets refuses to share the task of reducing short-term exchange rate

volatility and justifies its inaction on the specious grounds that it is improving the proper functioning of the market. No practical or intellectual support for the present official US position has ever been adduced, and should the present arrangements be recognized as harming US interests the policy would be changed. There is a difference between short-term limited intervention and the sort of action the US authorities were obliged to take until 1979 to support the dollar systematically and on a large scale. US aversion to intervention is the result of a dislike of continuing major intervention in either direction.

(2) Reducing the volatility of US interest rates is already an important Fed objective. There is an interesting contrast between continuing assertions that smoothing exchange rate operations hampers market operation and the willingness of the Fed to act on money markets against market pressures over a period of months. To the extent that the Fed succeeds in reducing interest rate volatility to that extent will an important short-term source of exchange rate instability be removed.

(3) If US interest rates were to increase from present levels (around 15 per cent in June 1982) for any sustained period, the consequences for both Euromarkets and the US domestic economy would almost certainly outdo most of the disaster scenarios at present being discussed in the USA. Many sovereign borrowers, including some of the largest, are finding their debt-servicing burdens almost insupportable because of the level of dollar interest rates and because of the short-term nature of the dollar debt available to them. Many US companies face similar problems with their debt structure for analogous reasons. Three-month Eurodollar interest rates at, say, 18 per cent and US prime bank rates at or above that level for months or a year would cause widespread defaults in Euromarkets and bankruptcies in the USA.

The margin between any given situation and calamity is, as a normal working assumption, a lot wider than writers of disaster scenarios are willing to believe. This may be true here too, but the Fed would be unwise to run the risks inherent in the experiment. Given the depth of the US recession and the continuing deceleration of US inflation, it is unlikely that pressures for increases in interest rates to previous peak levels will occur, especially for any significant period of time. Europe will have to hope that further US experiments in monetary management

45

will have a more pragmatic basis. It would undoubtedly be possible to find a monetary indicator that continued to suggest that interest rates should rise, and the continuing market nervousness about the behaviour of M1 shows that the task might be fairly simple. In the end monetary authorities cannot abnegate responsibility for monetary management to some arbitrary rule, for the 'auto-pilot' can steer a steady course straight for the rocks. The Fed, in the USA's interests as well as in Europe's, will have to accept its responsibility for the direct management of interest rates. This is becoming common ground in both Administration and Fed circles where there is general agreement that the level of US interest rates must fall. Monetary targets can survive in their present form only so long as the authorities make this aim clear.

(4) Any modifications in US monetary policy in the directions described above will, given the views of the Administration and the Fed, probably not be allowed to change the underlying restrictive stance of that policy. European monetary and exchange rate policies are evolving to accommodate a strong dollar even though this poses some adjustment problems, and they should welcome a continuing stable international monetary framework.

If these developments in US monetary policy — a lower level for interest rates, reduced interest rate volatility and a continuing conservative monetary stance — take place for domestic reasons, the next few years might see somewhat less turbulent foreign exchange markets than the beginning of the 1980s.

The objectives that Europe might set for itself would give the EMS a somewhat larger role than it has at present, but leave it far short of what its creators intended. These objectives would strengthen the existing zone of exchange rate stability within Europe and make management of EMS exchange rates against the dollar an explicit objective of European monetary policy. They depend on a general acceptance that exchange rate stability is sufficiently important to use interest rate policy to maintain it. This is accepted by the UK, is accepted reluctantly by West Germany and will only be accepted by France if it can use its exchange controls partially to insulate Euro–French franc rates against domestic interest rates. As for the willingness of the smaller EMS members to use interest rates to defend exchange rates, briefly: Italy is content to use interest rates to defend a periodically devalued lira; the Netherlands is happy with present interest rate policy; the Irish Republic is insulated by exchange controls, although it will be obliged to devalue sooner or later; Belgium is unwilling to defend its February 1982 rate against the Deutschmark but is eager to remain within the EMS at a rate it views as appropriate; Denmark is prepared to devalue periodically against the mark in line with its inflation differential to maintain competitiveness; and Luxembourg is considering ending its long-standing monetary union with Belgium because it does not wish to devalue against the mark, but remains the most convinced EMS member. The continuing existence of a broadly based EMS is, however, endangered by France's preference for domestic reflation over committed EMS membership.

As the Appendix notes, there is little evidence that short-term exchange rate volatility greatly disrupts trade and capital inflow. It is therefore reasonable to ask whether the interest rate fluctuations that would be necessary to maintain EMS exchange rates would be less troublesome than the exchange rate fluctuations that now occur. Under a system of adjustable peg exchange rates these fluctuations are limited, and the EMS has so far lived comfortably with them. The UK is already directing interest rates to an exchange rate target so that in its case the choice is between managing an effective exchange rate target and a Deutschmark target. The latter has the advantage that stable EMS rates would actually be recognized as such by traders, and this is not the case with a stable effective rate.

After the Versailles Summit

The meeting of the Heads of State of the major OECD countries in Versailles on 5 June was expected to devote most of its attention to the issues described in this book. In the event, developments in the Falklands and the Middle East largely diverted attention from the economic policy issues.

Before the Summit, widespread criticisms of US monetary policy, and of the extent to which the yen is undervalued, were expected. These were heard, but were muted and brought forth no convincing response from the American and Japanese governments. The USA was hardly in a strong position to criticize the weakness of the yen, since the Japanese authorities could rightly claim that this was largely a consequence of the level of American interest rates. European criticism of American monetary policy was tempered by the belief that the current level of interest rates now owes more to money market pressures and to fears about the prospective scale of US government deficit than to the policies of the Fed. The scale of the deficit was criticized.

Before the Summit, the American authorities had suggested that they would be willing to participate in a study of the advantages and disadvantages of intervention in foreign exchange markets to meet European criticisms of their present policy of total inaction. The Summit produced an agreement that countries would intervene as they saw fit to maintain orderly foreign exchange markets, but that they would not intervene to sustain exchange rates at unrealistic levels. This statement was sufficiently general to be interpreted in almost totally divergent ways by the countries present. French representatives commented that the USA had agreed to resume playing its part in foreign exchange market intervention. US representatives responded that they had been misunderstood and that, had the Versailles agreement on foreign exchange market intervention existed a year ago, their interpretation of it would not have required them to intervene in foreign exchange markets any more than they had done.

In fact the USA did intervene in foreign exchange markets for the first time since the March 1981 assassination attempt on President Reagan in the wake of the EMS realignments of June 1982. This too was justified by the need to calm markets given their unusual turbulence. It may, however, mark the beginning of a more active US exchange rate intervention policy which would be welcomed in Europe.

The Summit economic communiqué said: 'We are ready to strengthen our cooperation with the IMF in its work of surveillance and to develop this on a multilateral basis taking into account particularly the currencies constituting the Special Drawing Rights.' Some commentators saw this as placing a new emphasis on the role of the IMF through the 'Group of Five', the countries whose currencies make up the SDR: the UK, the USA, Germany, France and Japan. It is difficult to see what this will mean in practice. There were no indications in the discussions leading up to the Summit which suggested that any of the five saw any particular advantage in placing new emphasis on the IMF's role in stabilizing foreign exchange markets, nor any general belief that the

Fund could fulfil the role effectively.

In consequence, the summer of 1982 shows many signs of repeating the experiences of the preceding summer, with exchange rates moving sharply in markets where there is a low underlying level of transactions as people are reluctant to take views on their currency positions. The proposals for international monetary reform listed in this chapter, while modest and limited in their scope, are, seen from Versailles, far too ambitious.

And after the June EMS realignment

On Saturday 12 June there was another general EMS realignment, only eight months after the last one and four months after the Belgian devaluation. Its most noteworthy feature was the French franc's 10 per cent devaluation against the Deutschmark. This is larger than any previous single currency movement within EMS. It answers, for the time being only, one of the questions posed in this paper. France has chosen, and Germany permitted, a large devaluation as an alternative to a French withdrawal from EMS. There are suggestions that the price of German acquiescence was a reversal in the direction of French economic policy. It is unlikely that President Mitterrand will be able (or would wish) to adopt sufficiently restrictive policies to change the fortunes of the franc. The choice of a further devaluation or withdrawal from EMS will face the French authorities again in the near future. The Deutschmark and Dutch guilder were revalued against all other EMS currencies, not just the French franc. Such realignments will probably continue to be necessary at intervals of 6–12 months. EMS is thus developing into a *de facto* crawling peg system. The short-term stability EMS gives, together with the predictability of the exchange rate adjustments that occur, do offer a better framework for rational currency exposure management than the large, near-random moves of the dollar against the European currencies. A '*de facto*' crawling peg system may yet prove to be a practical mechanism for European exchange rate management.

Appendix: Exchange rate volatility and foreign trade

The following discussion of the effects of exchange rate volatility on foreign trade is based on three propositions:

(1)   exchange rate volatility adds to the risks faced by importers and exporters;

(2)   in consequence, foreign trade is reduced below the level it would have been had exchange rates been more stable; and

(3)   the development of forward markets in foreign exchange can reduce or eliminate foreign exchange risks and, in consequence, even extreme exchange rate volatility need not matter much.

On the key point, (2), there is an analytical problem: it is proper to ask 'reduce trade compared with what?' Under a fixed exchange rate regime a country with high domestic inflation will find that its exports become uncompetitive.This will generate a balance of payments crisis and may bring about the introduction of import controls in one form or another. Flexible exchange rates help free trade policies to be sustained. If governments had some objective measure of the appropriate levels for their exchange rates they might be able to engineer smooth moves from one exchange rate level to another, and so minimize foreign exchange risks. (Advocates of a crawling peg exchange rate regime would argue that such a system is possible as well as desirable.) Any exchange rate volatility beyond such moves generates uncertainty and obscures the information that exchange rates should give to market participants.

Exchange rate volatility increased in the 1970s and experienced a steep increase at the start of the 1980s. This volatility should have the effect of reducing foreign trade unless companies can insulate themselves against it because it makes the profitability of such trade so uncertain. It is difficult to find cases which support this contention, but there are companies that have reduced their overseas activities or abandoned them because of exchange rate volatility. British Leyland gave up some parts of the US car market because of a short period of sterling strength and Laker Airways ceased trading because of a continuing period of sterling weakness. In both cases exchange rate volatility was a contributory factor rather than the determining one, and it was not short-term fluctuations in the exchange rate that caused the problems but longer-term movements lasting for periods of months or years.

Well-developed forward markets enable companies partially to insulate themselves from foreign exchange fluctuations so that exchange rate volatility matters much less than it otherwise would. The extent to which companies can protect themselves is limited and the effective use of forward cover is difficult. It requires a coherent overall strategy which starts with properly specified objectives.

Suppose, for example, a UK company exports goods each month at a price of US $1,000. During 1981 a shipment would have fetched £417 in January, £550 in August and £505 in December if these receipts had been sold in the spot foreign exchange market. Suppose that the cost of the goods is £500 per shipment in the UK, then January's losses have to be financed by large August gains and much smaller December gains. Exporters seek to pass on foreign exchange fluctuations and so the assumption of a fixed price through the year is unrealistic — but not totally unrealistic if, for example, the price of these goods is constrained by the price of domestically produced goods in the USA, or the exporter quotes his price in dollars and can change it only at monthly or quarterly intervals.

Now consider the use of forward markets. If the exporter sells forward a year's worth of dollar receivables at the beginning of 1981 he ensures losses through the year by locking in at what proved, in retrospect, to be the highest level sterling reached that year in both spot and forward markets. He might, however, have wished to choose this option at the time on the expectation that sterling could have risen still higher. Obviously if the exporter sold forward the rest of the year's receivables in August he would have maximized the sterling value of his dollar receivables in the remainder of 1981. In August, however, sterling might have been expected to drop still lower and he might have preferred to continue exchanging dollar receivables in the spot market rather than the forward market. Like most financial decisions, hedging decisions are more easily made with hindsight!

Suppose that the exporter is going to continue earning US $1,000 of receivables each month through the indefinite future. Recognizing the uncertainties of exchange rate fluctuations he adopts a policy of selling them one year forward. He postpones the impact of each currency move by 12 months. This in itself may be useful (it helps financial planning to know the sterling value of receivables for the next year) but it does nothing to reduce the impact of exchange rate volatility on sterling income.

If the exporter in this simple example wants to reduce the volatility of his sterling income, and if he believes that the spot exchange rate will fluctuate randomly around the forward rate, then he will always sell forward *half* of his dollar receivables. This will more than halve the volatility of the exporter's dollar income when measured in sterling provided a complete cycle of appreciation and depreciation occurs within a year (the period of the cover), and it will have a worthwhile effect even if the cycle takes more than a year.

Appendix

There is a special category of cases in which forward markets become particularly useful. When a large 'one-off' contract involves currency receivables or payables whose amount and timing is known with certainty, forward markets give certainty about the value of the contract in the base currency of the importer or exporter. Cases such as this are special because they represent only a small proportion of international trade, but even here experience suggests that 'certain' payments have a habit of shifting in amount and timing to an extent that can make forward contracts almost as risky as leaving the initially projected exposure uncovered.

Participants in foreign exchange markets will have views on whether currencies are going to behave differently from the forward rates prevailing at any time. Given the magnitude of currency fluctuations, they will have an incentive to act to improve the value in their home currency of their foreign currency receivables. If they think their home currency will weaken against the currently available forward rate, instead of selling forward a 'neutral' 50 per cent of prospective receivables, they may sell forward some lesser proportion, or even none at all. If they believe their home currency will strengthen further they will sell forward more than the 'neutral' 50 per cent of prospective receivables to lock in the current favourable exchange rate. It is a reasonable operating maxim that anyone's foreign exchange forecasts will frequently be wrong so that doing either all or nothing in foreign exchange markets to cover currency exposures is generally unnecessarily aggressive.

It is worth emphasizing that a very large part of the flows of short-term funds across the exchanges can be generated by corporate treasurers changing their minds about a currency's prospects. If all UK importers come to believe that sterling is going to weaken sharply, they will buy forward their currency needs for the foreseeable future. At the same time UK exporters who share the same belief will desist from selling forward any of their currency receivables. In a really extreme case it would be possible to imagine importers paying for a year's imports in one day at the same time as all exporters postpone changing their currency receivables for sterling for as long as possible. Given that an amount equal to half UK GNP flows through sterling foreign exchange markets in payments for goods and services each year, even a limited change in foreign currency hedging strategies will cause large short-term capital flows. This is true in most countries now, and particularly in countries without exchange controls. It explains why direct intervention by central banks in foreign exchange markets is at present normally confined to smoothing operations, for the scale of flows through foreign exchange markets dwarfs the amount of reserves any monetary authority can spend to move an exchange rate. Official exchange rate policy now has to consist of an interest rate policy which changes the relative cost of hedging a currency.

Glossary

The glossary is intended to clarify the meaning of some commonly used economic and financial terms. It is not intended to offer precise operational definitions but to give a general understanding of what the terms mean.

adjustable pegged exchange rate. Following the agreement reached at Bretton Woods in 1944, exchange rates were pegged against the US dollar until 1973, when the system broke down. Subsequently, many currencies were allowed to float – that is, movements in their exchange rates were determined, at least in principle, by supply and demand in foreign exchange markets. Bretton Woods was a fixed-rate system; more specifically it was an 'adjustable' peg because a country could decide to revalue or devalue against the dollar. The EMS is in effect a system in which members of the European Community peg their exchange rates to the ECU. It is an adjustable pegged system because members change the fixed exchange rates at fairly frequent intervals. (Formally all member currencies are pegged against the ECU; in practice they behave as though they are pegged against the Deutschmark.)

bond prices and interest rates. If a $100 bond is issued at an interest rate of 10 per cent or US $10 a year, say, for the next 30 years, it will continue to sell at a price of US $100 while long-term interest rates remain at 10 per cent. If, to sell US $100 of long bond a year later, it is necessary to offer to pay US $20 a year, the interest rate is then 20 per cent. Clearly no one will wish to buy the bond paying US $10 a year until its price falls to around US $50. Then its yield will be equal to the yield on the bond paying US $20. Thus interest rates and bond prices are inversely related.

crawling peg exchange rate. When two countries, for example West Germany and Italy, have different rates of inflation, any fixed exchange rate will become out of date as, for example, Italian prices rise more rapidly than German prices. There are two solutions to this problem: periodic devaluations of the weaker currency's pegged exchange rate at intervals of, say, six months or a year; or – the crawling peg – frequent very small movements in the exchange rate of the weak currency against the strong currency, which compensate over time for the inflation differential.

Eurocurrency markets. Eurocurrency is foreign currency deposited with a bank outside the country where the currency is issued as legal tender; in the Eurocurrency markets foreign currencies are lent and borrowed mostly among banks and mostly at short term. The most important Eurocurrency is the Eurodollar, which accounts for about 80 per cent of the international capital markets' gross assets; other Eurocurrencies include the Eurodeutschmark, Euro–French franc and Eurosterling.

European Currency Unit (ECU). This is the currency unit of the European Monetary System (EMS) and in some respects resembles the SDR (*see* below). Created in 1979, it is a 'basket' currency. Its constituents are the currencies of the members of the European Community weighted roughly to reflect their relative importance. The ECU is an artificial reserve currency but is held only by central banks of EMS members.

Fed. An abbreviation for Federal Reserve System, which refers to the monetary authority of the United States. It has a number of components. US monetary policy is decided by the Federal Reserve Board operating with the advice of the Federal Open Market Committee (FOMC). The Federal Reserve System consists of twelve districts which cover the whole of the USA. Each district develops its own views on monetary policy and provides an input into the thinking of the Federal Reserve Board of Governors and the FOMC.

money supply (or *monetary aggregates*). The components of the money supply, categorized according to their liquidity, range from notes and coin at one extreme, to a wide range of interest-paying financial assets which can be sold to finance purchases by companies and individuals. The narrow definition of the money supply, M1, in the USA (and, indeed, in most other countries) consists of notes, coin, non-interest-paying current accounts and some interest-paying bank accounts, provided that cheques can be drawn on them at short notice. Wider definitions of money supply (M2, M3, etc.) include financial assets which have to be exchanged for money in its narrower sense before they can be used to finance purchases.

monetary targets. The Fed operates target ranges for the principal monetary aggregates (*see* money supply). The theory behind the policy of choosing to control the monetary aggregates is that there is a direct relationship between changes in nominal income and changes in the aggregates. There are two ways in which nominal income might grow more slowly: either the rate of inflation might fall or the growth rate of real income (output) might fall. The transmission mechanism from a restrictive monetary policy to constraints on nominal income and the relative effects on inflation and output (and hence employment) are subjects of continuing controversy among economists.

nominal and real interest rates. The nominal rate of interest is that actually quoted in the market. The real rate of interest adjusts this to take account of price inflation. In the common interpretation a nominal rate of interest of 15 per cent when prices are rising at 10 per cent per annum is equivalent to a real rate of interest of 5 per cent. But it can be argued that the appropriate adjustment would deduct the *expected* rate of price inflation over the period during which interest is to be paid.

reserve currency. The monetary authority of any country will wish to maintain foreign exchange reserves. By definition, it cannot hold reserves of its own currency as foreign exchange reserves. Countries tend to confine their holdings of foreign currencies to the major investment currencies: US dollar, sterling, Deutschmark, Japanese yen, Dutch guilder and French franc.

Special Drawing Right (SDR). The International Monetary Fund (IMF) created SDRs at the end of the 1960s as an artificial reserve currency issued by the IMF itself. It is now a 'basket' made up of five currencies: US dollar, sterling, Deutschmark, French franc and Japanese yen. Its value moves in line with the fluctuations in its component currencies. The basket is weighted to reflect roughly the relative importance in international trade and international financial markets of its constituent currencies.